'Great! A must-read if y...
into gospel-centred conv...

International President, Global Outreach Day

'Ben helps us practice and praise the divine strategy of using questions to advance the goodness of God.'

Danielle Strickland
Speaker, advocate and author

'Written by someone who has not just talked the talk, but has walked the walk – and it shows. Ben guides us brilliantly through some simple questions that could make evangelists of us all.'

Matt Redman
Worship leader, Grammy-winning songwriter and author

'This book is beautifully, winsomely, inspirationally and passionately crafted – read it and live it!'

Phil Knox
Evangelical Alliance and author, *Story Bearer*

'I'm so grateful for the way that Ben has challenged me in helpful ways to actively share my faith (and listen well!). This short book is invaluable to those wanting to grow in clearly communicating the best message.'

Sarah Yardley
Mission Lead, Creation Fest UK and author, *More Change*

'Give copies of this book to your whole congregation and help them go into the world with gospel confidence.'

Andy Hawthorne
Founder and CEO, The Message Trust

'This practical little book is an absolute gem. If you're looking to strengthen your evangelistic witness you must read it!'

Reuben Morley
Author, *The Introverted Evangelist*

'Through the art of asking questions, Ben unlocks how we can transform everyday conversations into extraordinary Gospel opportunities.'

Greg Stier
Founder, Dare 2 Share

'A very helpful book inspiring the messenger and honing the message. I loved it.'

Mark Greenwood
National Evangelist and Head of Evangelism,
Elim Pentecostal Churches UK

'What a great read! If you want to become better at sharing the greatest news in the world, you should definitely read this book.'

Graham Daniels
General Director, Christians in Sport

'In its beauty and simplicity, this book will help you to be clear and compassionate in every conversation, making the most of every opportunity.'

Desmond Henry
Director, Global Network of Evangelists

'We all know we should be sharing our faith, this unique and brilliant book shows us how to.'

Mark Ritchie
73rd Trust

'Sensitive and clear, thoughtful and practical. This honest guide to conversational evangelism is a great resource for anyone wanting to become more confident to share their faith.'

Andrew Ollerton
Author, *The Bible Course* and *The Bible:*
A Story That Makes Sense of Life

'This book will help you start good news conversations with those around you and help them step towards Jesus – read it, have a go and pass it on!'

Dr Rachel Jordan Wolf
Executive Director, HOPE Together

BEN JACK

IF JESUS IS THE ANSWER...

WHAT IS THE QUESTION?

TEN SIMPLE QUESTIONS FOR DYNAMIC EVANGELISM

© by Ben Jack 2021

Published by Equipping the Church, a brand of Kingsway CLC
Trust, Unit 5, Glendale Avenue, Sandycroft, Deeside, CH5 2QP

Kingsway CLC Trust is a registered Charity, Number
265612, and a Limited Company registered in registered
in England, Registration Number 1093879

Unless otherwise indicated, all Scripture references are taken from NIV:
New International Version® Anglicised, NIV® Copyright © 1979, 1984,
2011 by Biblica, Inc.® Used by permission, all rights reserved worldwide.

Concept development by The Message Trust
Cover design and typesetting by Simon Baker at Thirteen Creative
Author photograph by Rachael Silvester

Every effort has been made to ensure that this book
contains correct permissions and references, but if anything
has been inadvertently overlooked the Publisher will be
pleased to make the necessary arrangements at the first
opportunity. Please contact the Publisher directly.

Printed in the EU
ISBN: 978-1-83817-041-7

CONTENTS

CONTENTS

ADVANCE ESSENTIALS

Short, practical guides to help you effectively
proclaim the good news of Jesus Christ with
your lips and your life to the world around you.

INTRODUCTION

Conversations happen every day, which is probably why we've come to refer to them as 'everyday conversations'. Many of the Christians I talk with don't know how to turn their everyday conversations into opportunities to share the hope and joy of the gospel, even though they really want to. We know that Jesus is the answer to the hurt, brokenness and chaos of the world, but we are often unsure about how we can help people realise this for themselves. Inevitably, then, one of the questions I am asked most often when people find out that I'm an evangelist is what advice I can give to help them engage others in good gospel conversation.

Truth be told, there is no one-size-fits-all method for guaranteed success in personal evangelism ('personal evangelism' is the shorthand term we'll use in this book to mean having a conversation with a not-yet Christian about the gospel). Further, we should be wary of relying on an inflexible methodology that might work only in some situations – not least because, no matter how appropriate our method is, we can end up neglecting the power of God in favour of our own tried-and-tested techniques. Our methods won't save anyone, only Jesus can do that.

But so long as we are relying on God's power for the task of evangelism, it makes sense for us to be prepared for every situation, which is something the Bible specifically commands us to do (2 Timothy 4:1–2; 1 Peter 3:15). After all, while it is God who saves, it is also God who delights in using his people to be holy messengers to the world. We honour the responsibility he has given us by preparing ourselves to be better vessels through which he can work.

This little book explores five simple questions we can ask ourselves as we prepare to take the good news of Jesus into the world, and five dynamic questions we can ask the world as we go for his glory. By 'dynamic' I mean that these questions – and the conversations they lead to – are adaptable to the diverse people and situations we engage with. The idea is not to mechanically repeat these exact questions in every conversation you have about Jesus, but to use each one as a framework for conversation as you make the most of opportunities to turn the everyday into the extraordinary.

While it's a joy for me to pass on any wisdom and experience that could encourage you in your personal evangelism, this book is by no means a step-by-step guide to perfect evangelistic witness that will guarantee salvation for those you talk to. The ultimate fruit of your evangelistic witness (submission to the lordship of Christ, restored relationship with God, salvation) is in God's hands alone. However, the *success* of your evangelism is in your hands. That might sound like a contradiction, but only if you think that by 'success' I mean salvation fruit. I don't. The only success we can claim in evangelism is in being faithful to what God is asking us to do – to proclaim his good news with our lips and our lives by the power of his Holy Spirit (always the intended meaning of the word 'proclaim' in this book) to those around us every day (Matthew 28:16–20). You'll notice as you read that the stories I share don't always conclude with a neat 'salvation' ending – I've tried to include the good, the bad and the ugly in the hope that it will serve as an encouragement to you to think differently about what 'success' really means.

If this book helps you step faithfully – and, hopefully, more confidently – into gospel-centred conversations with those around you, then both this book and the evangelism you engage in can be considered a success. Thankfully, God has the rest in his unwaveringly faithful, powerful and loving hands.

PART ONE:
FIVE QUESTIONS FOR YOU

Before we run head-first into the world to ask the questions from the second half of this book, it is important that we first ask ourselves some simple questions to ensure our evangelistic witness is God-honouring, Jesus-centred and Holy Spirit-empowered. Here are five questions to help you reflect as you seek to be faithful to the gospel call of God in your life.

DO YOU KNOW THE POWER OF PRAYER?

The power of salvation belongs to God alone (Romans 1:16). No matter how gifted a conversationalist or communicator you may be, your verbal skills can't save anyone – only God can. If we want people to be impacted by the power of the gospel, we need to put the power where the power belongs: in the hands of God.

Growing up, I was obsessed with the 80s cartoon Masters of the Universe (which was essentially an extended toy advertisement). The hero, Prince Adam, would magically transform into the mighty He-Man by holding his trusty sword up to the sky and declaring, 'I have the power!' – at which point he would receive some kind of supernatural power with which he could fight against the villain Skeletor and his minions.

My wonderful grandmother bought me a replica He-Man sword so that I could run around the house, hold it aloft and receive 'the power' whenever my little heart desired (although I must confess I mainly attempted to use 'the power' to terrorise my sister). One day my grandmother came to visit and was delighted to see me proudly holding her gift above my head. She picked me up into her arms, but as she did I dropped the sword to the floor and began to cry inconsolably.

'What's the matter, darling?' She asked.

Through my tears as I looked down at my sword lying on the floor, I declared,

'I've lost the power!'

Whenever we fail to pray, we drop the sword. We lose the power. We put down our opportunity to be forgiven as we confess our sin, our potential to grow in maturity as children of God, and our way to be refined as obedient disciples of Jesus Christ (Matthew 26:41; Philippians 4:6; 1 Timothy 2:1–2; James 5:16). We forfeit the power by which God-given opportunities to witness to the world come into focus. We shake off the power of God at work in and through us and we shift our evangelism away from stirring hearts from death to life and towards merely 'marketing' the Christian faith (Colossians 4:2–6). We wave goodbye to the power by which we are emboldened and equipped with spiritual armour to defend against the attacks of the enemy and the fear of man as we step onto the frontline of spiritual battle (Ephesians 6:18).

I am convinced that the reason why many of our evangelistic opportunities go unnoticed or untaken, why conversations about Jesus go poorly, and sometimes why people fail to be persuaded by the truth of the gospel, is at least in part a lack of prayer by the very gospel messengers who are sent into the world in the Spirit's power.

United States Founding Father Benjamin Franklin reportedly once said, 'By failing to prepare, you are preparing to fail.' We prepare our hearts for evangelism through prayerful submission and petition to God. We could reframe the saying as:

'By failing to prayerfully prepare for evangelism, we are preparing to fail in evangelism.'

We must pray.

Pray for opportunity, pray for wisdom, pray for clarity, pray for salvation, pray for healing, pray for forgiveness, pray for discernment, pray for compassion, pray for boldness, pray to overcome the fear of man, pray for humility. Pray, pray, pray.

In the secret place, before you talk to anyone else about the King, talk to the King himself and seek his power for the task.

Of course, even with faithful prayer and a Spirit-empowered gospel message, people are still able to choose to reject the gospel. But we can trust God to be at work through our prayers, even when we don't always immediately see the outcome we might be hoping for (1 John 5:14–16). In fact, adopting an ongoing posture of prayer helps to remind us that evangelism is rarely (if ever) an event, but a journey in which we let God himself take the lead.

Prayer is not only part of our preparation, but is part of our action, too. While we are in an evangelistic conversation with people, we can also be in constant prayerful dialogue with God. I regularly find myself praying the following things internally while I'm talking to people about Jesus:

'Lord, thank you for this opportunity, please soften their heart to your gospel.'

'Jesus, please help me to speak clearly about your good news.'

'Would your joy be made clear in and through this conversation, Father.'

'Spirit, lead me to anything specific you want to say in this time.'

'Lord, would you give me your wisdom to answer this question.'

'God, would your glory be revealed in my weakness.'

Prayer can also be part of our personal evangelism as we offer to pray for others and let God work through those prayers. We'll pick this idea up again in Part Two, but, for now, take some time to reflect on the starting posture of our walk with Jesus and our proclamation of him into the world – on our knees before our King in faithful prayer, the fuel of our faith and the empowerment of our witness.

Commit to seeking the power and presence of God in prayer so that those you speak with may know his power and presence for themselves.

FURTHER REFLECTION

- Do I pray daily for my friends and family who don't yet know Jesus?
- Do I ask God for opportunities to share the gospel, and have I seen him provide them?
- Do I seek God's power for the opportunities he places before me, including boldness to overcome the fear of man?

DEEPER READING

- *How To Pray*, Pete Greig (Hodder & Stoughton, 2019)
- *Power Evangelism*, John Wimber (Hodder & Stoughton, 1985)

NEXT STEP

Create a prayer list of a few people in your life who don't yet know Jesus and commit to praying for them daily, that they would come to know him through your witness or any by any other means. You could also commit to prayer-walking the streets of your community regularly, asking God to move in your neighbourhood while making yourself available for him to answer that prayer through the interactions you have with the people you meet.

WILL YOU COMMIT TO KNOWING THE WORD?

I t's all too easy to hold back from engaging in conversations about our faith with those around us if we're not confident that we can explain what the gospel actually entails. None of us wants to be caught out because we didn't know something that we should, and surely it would be even worse to miscommunicate the gospel in a way that leaves someone with a false idea about Jesus and his good news. I heard from one person recently that, while they think evangelism is important, they don't personally get involved because they believe the gospel is far too precious to have a deficient person like them messing up its proclamation into the world.

And then there are other Christians who don't let such things hold them back (which in many ways is laudable), but because they themselves don't fully grasp the truth of the gospel, they can end up spreading confusion rather than clarity.

When I was a teenager, long before our current golden age of access to the Bible – with a plethora of mobile apps and resources to connect us to God's word at any time and in any place – I had to settle for a quirky little monthly devotional magazine aimed at young people. It was well-written, the design was engaging and the content helped me dig deeper into the Bible, but it never really made me want to go further in my reading than the short offering of the day. Despite our increased access to God's word today, the problem I had then is still the problem that many have now – all too often we don't make the time to read beyond a few verses and a short devotional paragraph.

Don't get me wrong – Bible devotionals can be helpful. I'm thankful that we have easy access to so many wonderful offerings from such a variety of godly men and women, and they're a great place to start. But if we want to know God more fully, and his gospel more deeply, we need to take time to luxuriate in scripture. It's time to stop taking short holidays into scripture, topping up our spiritual tan from the occasional ray of sunshine truth, and instead we must move into the neighbourhood of God's word – the only place where we can truly become part of his transformative community of truth.

When I began to take reading the Bible more seriously in my early twenties, it changed everything for me. It wasn't primarily out of a sense of Christian duty (although there's nothing wrong with discipline) but out of a desire to really get to know God. As well as discovering God's identity more fully and hearing him speak from the pages of scripture more clearly and more regularly, the truth of the gospel came into sharper focus in my life – intellectually, spiritually and practically.

Spending time in God's word will help you to understand the gospel truth you are proclaiming to the world. Many struggle to share the good news about Jesus simply because they don't understand it well enough for themselves. Study the Bible. Know God's word. Pray through scripture. Live by the truth of God's word, that you may proclaim him with your lips and your life.

Just like prayer, the Bible is also an evangelistic tool in itself. One recent study from Talking Jesus showed that more than a quarter of practising Christians regarded reading the Bible as a primary influence that led them to faith. As the Bible transforms us *for* evangelism, so it can also transform those who read it as part *of* our evangelism.

Don't settle for all-too-brief holidays in scripture. Instead, move in and dwell on God's word, so that you will be able to declare its truth more clearly to others. You don't need to become an academic scholar, but you do need to take the time every day to refresh your scriptural muscle memory, just like an athlete in the gym training for a big race. The race set before us is one of perseverance and faith that calls others into our joyful reality – knowing and loving our creator God.

Get to know God's word so that you and those you speak with may know him better.

FURTHER REFLECTION

- Do I have good habits for reading and engaging with the Bible?
- What do I enjoy most about reading the Bible and what do I find difficult?
- Do I understand the gospel well enough that I can explain it accurately and clearly? If not, what could I do to grow in my understanding?

DEEPER READING

- *The Bible: A Story That Makes Sense of Life*, Andrew Ollerton (Hodder & Stoughton, 2020)
- *How to Read the Bible for all its Worth*, Gordon D. Fee and Douglas Stuart (Zondervan, 2014)

NEXT STEP

Read the gospel of Mark over four days (four chapters a day) on repeat for a month. Keep a journal to record what you discover as you go, asking and answering these simple questions along the way:

- What did Mark want his readers to understand from these passages?
- How does this passage apply to my life today?
- What questions has this passage raised in me?
- What have I learned about God and his gospel from reading the Bible today?
- How might I explain what I'm learning clearly to someone else?

ARE YOU LEARNING TO LISTEN?

First dates throw up all kinds of concerns. What if I wear the wrong outfit? What if I get something stuck in my teeth? What if a nervous bladder requires an embarrassing number of trips to the bathroom?

These are all valid, but perhaps the biggest fear is that you won't have anything to talk about. After all, silence is awkward. Yet what can be even more dangerous than dwelling in the silence is trying to fill it. Before you know it, you'll have told an inappropriate joke, or spent the whole evening talking about yourself and accidentally shown yourself to be a narcissistic maniac. In our quest to eradicate the awkwardness of silence, we can easily saturate the air with nonsense, neglecting to create space to listen to the other person.

The same is true in our relationship with God. In our fast-paced world it seems that we have lost the ability – and maybe even the willingness – to really listen to God.

The Bible gives loads of examples of people making space for time alone with God, and chief among them is Jesus. He knew how important it was to hear from his Father for encouragement, refreshment, and instruction. His forty days in the desert, the time when he removed himself from the crowds (and his disciples) at Capernaum and his agony in the garden of Gethsemane before his arrest all reveal a Jesus who placed an extremely high value on prayer and solitude with his Father. During these so called 'wilderness' experiences it's no stretch to imagine Jesus spending time in silence, patiently and attentively waiting on the precious and powerful voice of the Father.

We might assume that our mouths are our primary tool for evangelism, but the truth is that our ears are just as essential. We first listen to God through prayer and study of his word so that we would come to know his gospel more fully, hear his call on our lives more clearly and respond accordingly. But we must also listen to those we speak with.

What is their story?

What are the concerns and challenges they are facing?

What has taken the place of Christ in their lives?

Don't assume you know the answers to these questions before you have taken the time to listen and discover. It's no use trying to give a drowning man a cup of water to quench his thirst. Correctly concluding that he needs rescuing is not enough. Using your senses to determine how best to help him is crucial, or even your most enthusiastic rescue efforts will still leave him drowning.

I have often waded into conversation with a little too much enthusiasm for 'getting Jesus in' only to realise the other person has glazed over and lost interest because I exhibited so little interest in them.

On one occasion I was sat in a park in New York City when a young man approached me.

'Are you in music or film?' he asked (I'm not sure what this says about my look other than the possibility that one day I'll have to start dressing my age). I laughed and explained that although I was a DJ, I actually thought of myself as an evangelist first and foremost.

'Oh, what's that?' he replied.

Boom.

No doubt entranced by my British accent (my greatest asset whenever I'm stateside), he had walked head-first into my evangelism trap. I had him now.

Cut to five minutes later, and I'm giving him both barrels of my best gospel presentation. But just as I was hitting full flow, he held up his hand and stopped me in my tracks.

'I don't want to talk about this anymore.'

Oh.

We sat in silence for a moment, and then he politely said goodbye and walked away. I was thoroughly disappointed (and nursing a bruised ego). What had gone wrong? He had asked me a question and I'd seized the opportunity. Isn't that what we're supposed to do?

The young man wanted someone to talk to during his lunch break and stumbled across me in the park – someone who looked like a peer, a good conversation partner. But instead of having a conversation with him and finding out about his life, I'd just preached at him. He soon lost interest and the moment was gone.

He wasn't the one who had walked straight into an evangelism trap, I was. I'd fallen into the trap of putting preaching before person. It's hard to help someone discover the truth that God loves them when his ambassadors seem disinterested in them.

As well as the biblical examples of people listening to God, there are also plenty of examples of people *being listened to*, that they might come to a deeper understanding of who God is in response. Reflect upon Jesus in his interactions with Nicodemus, the Samaritan woman, or Cleopas and his buddy on the road to Emmaus (John 3; John 4; Luke 24:13–27). Jesus was the master of personal evangelism, not least because he knew when to ask and when to answer, when to speak and when to listen. We can certainly learn from his example, and what's more we are empowered with the gift of his heavenly wisdom by the Holy Spirit.

Just like Jesus, then, ask good questions and listen to the answers given. We don't just listen so that we have reference points for connecting a person's life to the gospel, we listen because we love those we speak to as God does. In listening we develop kinship, affinity, awareness, compassion, and clarity. And our responses should not be pre-determined evangelistic statements, but authentic acknowledgements of the stories they share, the challenges they face, the concerns they have, the idols they hold and are held by. It's only in light of these things that we might suggest to them that Jesus is indeed the answer.

All of this listening is to be rooted in our understanding of the gospel (so get reading!) and the Lord's leading (so get praying!) as we open ourselves up to listening to him during our conversations with others.

Listening. The best kept secret in evangelism.

FURTHER REFLECTION

- Do you find it easy or difficult to spend time silently alone with God? Why is this?
- What does it mean to 'listen' to God?
- How can you develop your listening skills so that you listen well to others, especially when you are keen to tell them about Jesus?

DEEPER READING

- *You're Not Listening*, Kate Murphy, (Vintage, 2020)
- *Confronting Christianity*, Rebecca McLaughlin (Crossway, 2019)

NEXT STEP

Think about how you can be more present in conversations and become better at listening in general. Take a friend to dinner and leave your phone in the car. Engage that outspoken work colleague in conversation, but resist the urge to interject or interrupt – let them make their full point, then go away and think about what they have said instead of responding there and then. Call someone you haven't spoken to in a while, ask them to share their news and sit back and take it all in. Most importantly of all, prioritise that solo silent time each day to sit at the feet of your heavenly Father. Ask him to speak to you, and *listen*.

CAN YOU GET BETTER WITH PRACTICE?

O nce, while I was waiting for service in a hotel bar, I noticed an elderly lady on crutches and in a neck-brace sitting alone and looking decidedly miserable. Being the cheery evangelist that I am, I decided to spark up conversation with her in an attempt to make her evening a little more pleasant, and maybe even open up an opportunity to share the love of Jesus with her. I began with the words, 'Have you been in the wars, my love?' In hindsight, I'm not sure I could have been more patronising. But there I was, hoping she would have an opportunity to tell me about her recent fall, to which I could respond with the requisite compassion and concern. Instead, her stony reply came: 'No, I have spinal arthritis.'

I hadn't expected that. A twisted ankle, sore back or dodgy hip would each have been acceptable responses but for some reason I wasn't anticipating such a grim diagnosis. This curveball threw my brain into panic, and seeing as my mouth struggles to listen to my brain at the best of times, cooperation between the two ceased. All I could manage in reply was the frankly hideous question, 'Oh… does that get better in the sunshine?'

I know, I know. I have no idea what I was thinking. She looked at me as if I had just thrown her cat out of the window and replied with a suitable amount of venom, 'It never gets better!'

There ended our conversation, although not our awkwardness – later on we ended up in the same lift together before getting off at the same floor. For a brief horrible moment, I thought she was going to follow me back to my room to beat me up with her crutches, which under the circumstances would have been fair enough.

It might seem strange or even insincere to rehearse potential evangelistic conversations, but, if you are not naturally comfortable talking with people about Jesus, then a little practice with friends can help a lot. Play out different situations, objections, questions and possible curveballs that might come up so that you have a little extra experience in knowing the ways you could respond appropriately. Not only will this help you to explain the gospel with more clarity, but it will reduce the chances that you end up on the back foot, becoming defensive or losing your cool. After all, almost as important as the truth and accuracy of what we say is the way in which we say it.

Clarity doesn't only hinge on using the right words, analogies or cultural connection points. It is also affected by the tone in which we speak. We don't need to become supreme masters of communication, but it's easy enough to knock off a few rough edges here and there so that others can understand our message – and hopefully our hearts – more clearly.

Also, pay attention to those around you who are great conversationalists, and, if possible, find an opportunity to be with them during a moment of personal evangelism. The disciples had a front row seat for most of Jesus' conversations, and watching the master at work would have made them even more effective communicators about him – in part because of what they witnessed from his life as they became witnesses to his life. We too can learn from the master as we read God's word and reflect on Jesus' ministry, and we can learn from others as we see the way they approach their own conversations about him.

If you are a church leader, I wonder how you help your congregation to practice their evangelism. Do you devote time to this as part of your Sunday services from time to time, perhaps by asking people to share their faith with the person seated next to them? I know a number of churches where this has radically increased people's confidence in evangelism. And when you make space for sharing testimonies, do you make space for stories about evangelism, even when it hasn't gone to plan? Testimony brings encouragement and inspires faith – and that's not just reserved for the stories with a neat ending! The more we can celebrate simple obedience in our church communities, the more we'll see our shared confidence grow.

Even with practice you can never foresee every possibility, and, just like my unfortunate hotel encounter, there will always be conversations and situations that take you by surprise. But practice can really help build your confidence in dealing with the most unexpected conversational turns, and give you a better shot at keeping Jesus at the centre of everything you say.

Practice doesn't always make perfect, but it can help you communicate his perfection more clearly.

FURTHER REFLECTION

- Do you find talking to people about your faith intimidating? If so, why?
- How can you be more aware of your tone in conversations, for example when talking about something that makes you a little defensive? How can you manage it better?
- What areas of conversation do you think it would be most helpful for you to 'rehearse' with a friend?

DEEPER READING

- *Stay Salt*, Rebecca Manley Pippert, (Good Book Company, 2020)
- *How To Talk About Jesus (Without Being That Guy)*, Sam Chan (Zondervan, 2020)

NEXT STEP

Ask a Christian friend or two to play through some conversations with you, and to deliberately throw you some curveballs. Get comfortable with strange things coming up in conversation – questions you can't answer right away, hostility, dismissiveness and so on. Working through a few scenarios with your friends will definitely make one or two encounters less intimidating in the future.

HAVE YOU CONSIDERED THE NEXT STEPS?

I'm not really an outdoors-y type. Most of my friends enjoy heading out into the countryside for long walks but I'm much happier in my local coffee house or cinema. That being said, to avoid being a complete nature Scrooge, I will occasionally venture to the great outdoors. On those rare occasions I put myself at the mercy of my friends to plot a route that will result in a nice day out rather than a body-punishing trek.

Now and then, these walks involve a little bit of climbing. It's never anything too taxing, but enough of an incline to require careful placement of my feet so as to avoid certain death (well, a sprained ankle at least). In these moments I often find myself asking, 'Where next?' and, usually, my friends are kind enough to ignore my persistent moaning and help to direct my steps. But can you imagine if they took me to the top of a tricky summit only to abandon me there with little hope of finding my way back down safely? It would be reckless and cruel. If my friends take me up, it's their responsibility to make sure I can get back down again.

Unfortunately, many view sharing the gospel as a task that is complete once someone has put their hand up during an altar call or prayed some kind of 'sinner's prayer'. It as if we've walked them to the summit and decided 'mission accomplished'. From there it's 'Good luck and goodbye, I hope you get on okay in whatever follows, but I've got more people to bring up here.'

Jesus was the master of evangelism and of discipleship. There's a lot more going on in the magnificent scene of his transfiguration than we can talk about here, but one thing that always strikes me is how keen the disciples are to stay up there in the splendour of this glorious experience, in stark contrast to how keen Jesus is to get back down into the reality of life in the valley (Matthew 17:1–8, Mark 9:2–8, Luke 9:28–36). From the disciples' point of view, they've just witnessed something heavenly and wondrous, so it's no surprise that they might want to dwell in the moment for as long as they can. But Jesus had a mission to accomplish and wanted to get back to his Father's business. This is a lesson for us all.

As witnesses of God's glory, our goal (figuratively at least) is to guide people to the mountaintop where they can see Jesus for who he is in all his splendour. But once they have recognised that he is indeed Lord and that they should trust him as such, down the mountain we must come to live in the reality of the lives that God has called us to. We are to go into the valley to die with Christ and become new creations for his glory (2 Corinthians 5:17).

It is vital, then, that we consider what will happen next when we are explaining the gospel to someone. If they encounter Christ there and then, what are we going to do? Pat them on the back and walk away? The sad truth is that far too much of our evangelism does essentially end in this way. I'm not sure if it's due to low expectations, a failure to properly prepare, or a lack of understanding on the part of the witness, but people are too frequently left to fend for themselves as soon as they've made a 'decision'.

Tragically, I suspect that there are many who have been both 'won' and 'lost' on the same day thanks to some great evangelism followed by no thought about what comes next. In fact, let me correct that statement: there is no such thing as 'great evangelism' that lacks a good follow up plan. For our evangelism to be great, it needs to provide a way by which a brand-new Christian can go on to live for Jesus as his disciple. A decision to follow Jesus should not be an arbitrary agreement with a set of doctrinal propositions, but a commitment to life in relationship with and submission to him. We cannot abandon people at the mountaintop. We need to help them, directly or indirectly, to walk next into the valley of Christian life.

Do you have a way by which you could engage someone personally in their ongoing walk with Jesus, or a connection with a local person or church who could if you cannot? If they commit to Christ there and then, what will the next step be? An introduction to Christianity like The Alpha Course or Christianity Explored? A connection to a local church, or even your own? A meet up for coffee the next day? Are you prepared to be flexible to meet their needs, even if it means introducing them to another Christian who might be better placed to journey with them than you?

Every opportunity for personal evangelism should lead to a next step, so that even when your conversation ends, their journey with Jesus doesn't.

FURTHER REFLECTION

- If someone chose to follow Jesus through a conversation with me today, do I know what the next step could be for them on their journey of discipleship?
- Where does my responsibility for someone's journey of faith start and end?
- What does it mean for me to take discipleship as seriously as I take someone's initial decision to follow Christ?

DEEPER READING

- *Basic Christianity*, John Stott (IVP, 2008)
- *The Masterplan of Evangelism*, Robert E. Coleman (Baker, 1963)

NEXT STEP

Make a list of local churches with some basic information about them, such as where they are and what time their services start. Look into who is running The Alpha Course or Christianity Explored locally. Find out which groups your own church offers for different age groups, interests, and so on (and if there is not much happening, perhaps chat with your leadership about how you could help to get something going that might be a good first step for a new believer). Preparation in these areas will mean that, as you engage in evangelistic conversations, you'll already know how best to support someone who might express further interest or choose to follow Jesus.

PART TWO:
FIVE QUESTIONS
FOR THE WORLD

We could certainly ask more questions in our personal evangelism than the five that follow. And while it's unlikely that every one of them would feature in every conversation, these five dynamic questions – dynamic in the sense that you can easily adapt them to any situation – are a good starting point for authentic Christ-centred conversations that treat others not as evangelistic 'targets' but as people who are deeply loved by God.

THE GOSPEL HEART QUESTION

'HOW ARE YOU?'

I know what you're thinking: *I've just bought a book about questions I could use in my personal evangelism and the best this guy can come up with is, 'How are you?'*

While you might not need a doctorate in Social Science to recognise the value of such a question in daily life, it can be all too easy to dismiss this question as too obvious or too trivial. 'How are you?' is often used as a casual greeting rather than a genuine question, and most of the time we would find it strange if the other person responded with a detailed explanation of their emotional state or current circumstances. However, dismissing this basic question is to miss a golden opportunity for evangelism – specifically because it reveals our gospel heart when we ask it with sincerity.

'How are you?' is more than a polite conversation starter. It is a way that we can start a conversation by saying something very important up front: I care about you.

There's no hidden tactic here. We should ask people this question because we genuinely care about how they are! People are not evangelistic targets, they are the beloved creation of God, and he cares about every detail of their lives (Genesis 1:26–31; Psalm 139; Luke 12:6–7). As God's ambassadors, we take an interest in a person's life to show that God – and we as his transformed people – care deeply about them. And the wonderful thing about a basic question like this is that the answer can often reveal connection points that can open up a gospel-centred conversation (and opportunities to offer practical support) through which we can demonstrate God's loving care more fully in word and action as the conversation or relationship progresses.

Another great way to frame this question is to invite someone to tell you their story. If 'How are you?' unlocks the other person's immediate state of mind, emotion, or circumstance, then 'Would you tell me your story?' provides an opportunity to explore the bigger picture of their life journey. Not everyone will be in the right frame of mind to answer this question – so it's important to exercise some level of discernment – but you may be surprised how often people will be willing to share their story with you if you take the time to listen. I have certainly been encouraged by how often this kind of story sharing opens up opportunities for the gospel to be explored and explained in response.

But it's not always our job to make the first move – great news for those of us who are a little conversation-shy! There are times when others will start the conversation for us, perhaps to request our help in some way. When these opportunities arise, we can respond from that same place of care and interest in the other person's life by meeting any practical need we can, and engaging in gospel-centred conversation as we do. If we truly care about the person in front of us, it will not be enough simply to offer practical help and leave their spiritual need unmet. Similarly, telling them about Jesus while, for example, not giving them the food they need to eat that day would be somewhat tone-deaf.

Meeting practical needs is not a one-way street when it comes to evangelism. When Jesus met the Samaritan woman at the well, he didn't ask what he could do for her, but instead asked her if she could help him because he was thirsty (John 4:7–42). From this simple (albeit culturally inappropriate) request, Jesus led the woman to the truth, and she became an immediate ambassador for him as she ran to tell everyone in her town about her encounter.

If we can learn to ask the right questions, listening to God even as we listen to the other person, then even when we are the ones in need we can still demonstrate our eternal hope in God as he works in and through us to be a witness of his love and care.

Once, I was shopping in a supermarket in Brooklyn when an elderly lady approached me and asked if I could help her out. She didn't have enough money to buy a few essential food supplies and she wondered if I would help her to afford a couple of extra tins of food. I happily agreed to help her on one condition – that she would help me find tin foil. This was both an excuse to extend our time together so we could have a nice chat, and also a helpful solution to my increasingly desperate search for an item which seemed to be as well-concealed as the Holy Grail.

She responded at the top of her voice, 'Oh Lordy! I don't even know what that is! But I'mma help you find it!' before rushing off down the aisle declaring to any and all with ears in the tri-state area, 'I need help here, someone come help me here.'

Thankfully she quickly explained to the store assistant that I needed help finding something called 'tin foil', and their initial concern that I was trying to attack her swiftly disappeared. A quick clarification about the British name 'tin foil' and the US name 'aluminum foil' later, and I was fully-equipped for my barbecue while my new shopping buddy was well on her way to a fully-stocked cupboard. We'd managed a lovely conversation about how God provides – a truth with which she enthusiastically agreed while stacking more and more tins of mackerel into her basket. She disappeared out of the store while I was paying at the checkout and I didn't see her again, so I have no idea what impact our encounter might have had in that dear lady's life, but I know that God is faithful in all our efforts, beyond what we see first-hand. Nothing is wasted in the economy of God's mission.

Never underestimate the relational and spiritual power of that simple question, 'How are you?' when we ask it with God's sincere care for the other person . As Jesus is revealed in our lives through simple 'gospel heart' questions of care (and our actions to meet the practical needs in front of us), so may he then be lovingly proclaimed from our lips in the conversation or relationship that follows.

GOSPEL HEART QUESTIONS

- What's going on in your world at the moment?
- Would you tell me your story?
- Is there anything you need? How can I help?
- Has anything good happened in your life recently?
- What is the biggest challenge you are facing right now?

THE GOSPEL IDOL QUESTION

'WHAT IS THE MOST IMPORTANT THING IN YOUR LIFE?'

One of the most striking stories we find in the Gospel accounts comes from Jesus' encounter with a rich young man (Matthew 19:16–30; Mark 10:17–31; Luke 18:18–30). Having heard about the teaching and wisdom of Jesus, this wealthy young man seeks him out so that he can ask an important question: 'How can I receive eternal life?'

The world's wealthiest people are still asking that question today. Many are throwing billions of dollars at medical and technological research in an attempt to help them live longer. But even the richest people in the history of the world haven't yet been able to buy their way out of the inevitability of death.

Jesus' response to the young man's enquiry is simple: keep God's laws, live as he requires, and you'll qualify for eternal life. With the kind of staggeringly-confident swagger that would befit a heavyweight boxer staring down a toddler in the ring, the young man assures Jesus that the commandments are in full unbroken order in his life.

Jesus doesn't bat an eyelid at the young man's misplaced confidence – or more accurately, his lie. Instead, Jesus sees beyond the swagger and into what occupied the throne of the young man's heart: his wealth.

Wealth gave the young man his status, his security – and if his response to Jesus about the commandments is a clue – his overconfidence. Money was the lord of his life. And as Jesus sees the idol at the centre of the young man's life, he is filled with love for him.

Jesus replies, 'Okay then, if you keep all the commandments, the only other thing you need to do is to go and sell everything you have, and give all your money to the poor.'

The young man is stunned. He turns from Jesus and walks away in disappointment.

If we're not careful, we can leave people with the idea that Jesus is just one good option among others for self-improvement, as if he is yet another wise guru dispensing ancient yet timeless advice. Aside from the fact that it's categorically untrue, this idea plays unhelpfully into the common objection: But I'm a good person, I do good things and try not to hurt anyone, why wouldn't God let me into heaven? This seems to be how the rich young man approached Jesus. But Jesus is not a mere dispenser of advice about ways to make our lives better, he is the way to the only true life – eternal life (John 14:6). When the young man realised the cost attached to knowing true life, he had nothing left but disappointment because he couldn't conceive of paying such a price. His idol was too entrenched upon the throne of his life to make space for the true king, Jesus.

Our conversations must not simply lead people to think that Jesus will make their lives better. We are not pointing to self-improvement but self-denial through Jesus' work upon the cross (Matthew 16:24–26). It is a difficult and costly message: what could cost us more than acknowledging that Jesus is Lord and we are not?

The gospel message is undoubtedly one of love, peace, hope, reconciliation and salvation (John 3:16; Romans 15:13; Colossians 3:15; 1 Peter 1:3; 1 John 4:9–10). But the true heart of the gospel is God's holiness, and his desire for us become a holy people who will give glory to and inherit his holy kingdom (Leviticus 11:45; 1 Peter 1:15–16).

We should be careful not to offer a well-intentioned but deficient gospel message that says: Jesus is love, and if you accept his love you can know eternal life after death.

The true gospel is far better than that: Jesus is Lord, and when you accept his Lordship you will know his eternal love and life both today and forever.

This is no 'cosy' love with a cherry-on-top assurance of a pleasant afterlife, but the powerful reality of the loving Lordship of Jesus. It's a revelation that God loves us deeply, but that we have run far away from his care, his power, and his right to rule our lives as the only one qualified to do so. In running away we have chosen death, but by turning back to God through trusting and submitting to Jesus as Lord, we can know true life. This is no oppressive subjugation of slave by master, but the freedom-ensuring submission of a willing heart before God. He created us to be holy, and by submitting to him we are choosing to partner with him in the refining process of being made holy, that we would truly be his image bearers into the world.

From this perspective our message to the world is this: he who formed the heart that beats in your chest today desires to form it afresh now in the image of his perfectly good, loving and holy character. He desires to know you, sustain you, empower you, and refine you into the life you were created for, a holy life of worship that brings him glory. And as we turn from trying to form our own hearts our own way – which only ever damages them – to embracing his love and forgiveness, it's a process that starts today and finds its perfection in eternity.

That is what eternal life really looks like, and there's only one way to it. To get rid of the false king on the throne of our lives and let the true King reign.

Like it or not, we all enthrone something at the centre of our lives. It makes perfect sense: we were created to worship God, but when that worship isn't pointed towards him it's going to end up pointed elsewhere. We can't help it. And while in many cultures explicit idolatry – the kind we see throughout the Old Testament – is still prevalent, in the Western world it's often more subtle. We'll certainly rub shoulders with those from other faiths and have the opportunity to learn about their cultural and religious experiences, and in those cases the more we can commit ourselves to the ideas in the first part of this book (prayer, the Bible, practice, knowing the next steps and, crucially, listening) the better. But there are many who are primarily devoted not to a particular deity or worldview but to something else entirely. In other words, there's always something that everyone would consider to be the 'most important thing' in their life.

Asking, 'What is the most important thing in your life?' can be awkwardly direct, so it is worth thinking about how you might include it in a regular conversation. I remember a very chatty lady who I spoke with for a couple of hours on a train journey, who made it clear to me that her children were everything to her. She was a divorcee who hated to interact with her ex-husband, yet she did so regularly because it was important for the kids. She expressed, 'He's their dad, they love him and he should be part of their lives.' Her children were so precious to her that she was prepared to face personal discomfort and make sacrifices to ensure they could flourish.

Conversations like this offer so many natural opportunities to introduce truths about God's character. Imagine this: 'So your kids are the most important thing in your life? It sounds like you would do anything to make sure they were safe and could flourish, no matter the cost. That's wonderful! Actually, I think you feel that way because you are made in God's own image, and God loves his kids too. But God is heartbroken that his children have run away from his perfect love and away from his care, and so he has done something to bring us safely home...'

From there, you could tell them the parable of the prodigal son (Luke 15:11–32). You could reflect upon God as a perfect Father (Matthew 5:48, 6:26; Luke 6:36; James 1:17; 1 John 4:16). You could talk about the saving work of Jesus, God's Son (Romans 5:8). The simple fact that a parent loves their kids opens up so many gospel opportunities! I'm sure I don't need to do all the evangelistic maths for you before you can see how we might find opportunities to connect the other person's story to God's story.

I took the opportunity to make that kind of gospel connection with the lady on the train and we had a great conversation. She was moved by my offer to pray for her family and her parting words to me as I arrived at my stop were so encouraging:

'You really believe what you say, don't you. I think you could do some real good with that, and we need all the help we can get!'

Not fully getting it yet. No tearful prayer of repentance. No revival breaking out in the train carriage. Just an ordinary mum beginning to think about what it would mean for her and those she loves if we really were children of God. Lord, would you please water that seed and let it grow.

Sometimes, it might be appropriate to gently point out the deficiencies of certain idols in a person's life. Money, career, possessions, status and comfort (among other things) can all come and go, but Jesus is the firm foundation upon which to build true life.

Of course, not everything we prioritise in our lives are idols, and most of what we do turn into idols are not evil in and of themselves. Family is a wonderful thing. Pursuing a career can be fulfilling, purposeful and godly. Money can be used to bless and be a blessing. But anything that is allowed to ascend the throne of our lives and usurp Jesus from his rightful place is an idol that will – if left unchecked – distract, distort and even destroy our relationship with him. There is only one true God, and we are to love him with everything we are (Deuteronomy 6:4–5). As we identify any idol in a person's life, we should be filled with love for them as Jesus was with the young man – a love that leads to compassionate questions, clear answers, and a Christ-centred invitation to enthrone the King of kings.

Our conversations with those around us would do well to help people reflect on who or what is seated on the throne of their life. Let us redeem the good things under the guidance of the King in his rightful place, and cast away the things that have no place in the fullness of life that God created us for. As we ask questions with compassionate love, wisdom, discernment, gentleness and humility, may our conversations help people to move from disappointment to true life.

GOSPEL IDOL QUESTIONS

- Are you a person of faith?
- What's your biggest dream in life?
- If your house was on fire, what's the one thing you would rescue?
- If you won the lottery, how would you spend the money?
- What do you think is the meaning of life?

THE GOSPEL PROBLEM QUESTION

'IF YOU COULD ASK GOD A QUESTION, WHAT WOULD IT BE?'

Have you ever had a conversation with someone where it seemed like the deck was stacked against you? I've had a fair few conversations over the years that were going well right up until the point the other person discovered I was a Christian, or we hit upon a certain aspect of the gospel that they weren't comfortable with. On those occasions you quickly sense that something has shifted. In many of these conversations we were able to keep talking and I discovered the source of the shift: a bad church experience, a religion-caused family rift, a deep-rooted objection to something that the Bible teaches, or an underlying feeling that they must be talking to a moron (though there's always the chance that feeling was prompted simply by being in conversation with me).

Even the most open-minded and faith-sympathetic not-yet-Christians have questions and concerns about God, faith and Christianity. For that matter, so do I! The moment we engage someone in a conversation about Jesus, we must be ready to hear about any of their barriers to faith. Peter famously exhorts us to, 'Always be prepared to give an answer to everyone who asks you to give the reason for the hope that you have. But do this with gentleness and respect' (1 Peter 3:15). We have a responsibility to be prepared to explain who is the source of our hope and why we have put our whole trust in him. Along the way we may discover that people think it is absurd, objectionable, laughable, baffling, intriguing and so on, but as we meet these reactions we have an opportunity to gently uncover the root of these concerns or objections. There's almost always more to the story than what first meets the ear.

We could think about it like this. We stand with a bare-footed not-yet-believer at the top of a long road. At the far end of the road is the cross of Christ. But the road is littered with potholes, blockages, walls, debris and sharp objects. The cross itself is barely visible through a haze of fog. Part of our evangelistic task is to do anything and everything we can to spiritually, intellectually, emotionally and practically help the person continue their journey along the road. We must attempt to sweep away debris, fill in potholes, tear down walls, remove any blockages and clear the fog. Our ultimate goal is to help the person get closer to the cross, for it is there that they will encounter Jesus, behold his saving work and have the opportunity to know true life through putting their trust in him. Don't forget that the power of salvation is in God's hands – it's still true that no-one was ever reasoned into the kingdom of God by having all their objections dealt with on an intellectual level. But in dealing with the other person's objections seriously, we might clear the road a little more, paving the way for them to become more open to encountering God's saving power for themselves.

The problem raised by the other person might not be an intellectual objection, but a very real and present challenge in their life that they cannot reconcile with the idea of a God who cares about them. This raises an important question for us as we reach out to the world: is it okay to use someone's present trouble as an opportunity to share the gospel? The distinction lies in the difference between exploitation and exaltation.

If we were trying to sell something to someone, it might be exploitative to use a difficult time in their life for our profitable advantage, unless of course the product we sold them could directly help in their present struggle. But we are not salespeople. We are the messenger children of God who are bringing his good news to the world. To point to Jesus in the midst of a crisis is not exploiting the person to whom we speak, it is exalting the person of whom we speak – Jesus – so that the other person may know his power, peace, love and hope in their life.

By the way, don't worry about needing to have a perfect response to every possible intellectual question or emotional objection you might encounter. Sometimes the barriers to faith we come across feel overwhelmingly unsolvable and leave us feeling way out of our depth in the conversation. But even if you could answer every question perfectly, it wouldn't necessarily result in the other person choosing to put their trust in Christ. I'll say it again: no-one was ever reasoned into the kingdom of God.

I was once having a conversation with a friend who was an atheist exploring various objections to faith in God. At the end of our discussion, he looked at me and said with absolute sincerity, 'You're really good at this, you know what you're talking about. You've thought about this a lot more than me, answered all my questions thoroughly, and I am sure that you really believe what you say…'

There was a pause. He shifted a little in his chair. He didn't want to cause offence and he wanted me to know that I had done a good job, that I shouldn't feel responsible for what was coming next…

I smiled and helped him along, 'But…'

He sighed. 'But I just can't believe it's true.'

We must resist the temptation to reduce our evangelism to this equation:

clever answer × as many as needed = salvation

None of us chose to follow Christ because we heard clever answers, we put our trust in Jesus because he knocked on the door of our lives and we responded by letting him in as Lord.

We should listen carefully to the questions and objections we meet and offer responses as we feel able and as the Spirit leads, but we should never be afraid to say 'I don't know'. We know the source of all truth in Jesus, but that doesn't mean we have it all perfectly figured out and can offer a perfect answer every question. It often means we have just enough knowledge to trust in him today. Never be afraid to take time to consider your response to a question or objection – silence is rarely as awkward as you suspect, and usually shows the other person that you are really listening to them.

More than it simply being the truth, saying 'I don't know' can even help lead to setting up another conversation with the other person. You could say, 'That's a great question... I don't really know much about that, maybe I could go away and think about it and we could meet again sometime?'

More often than not, the other person will be touched by your willingness to engage in this humble and intentional way, and they're likely to be curious enough to take up your offer. My friend has told me on more than one occasion that he simply can't believe that God is real, despite acknowledging that he has received many good answers to his questions over the years. And yet he still regularly asks me questions about faith. Jesus is still knocking on the door of his life. Good answers may help my friend journey towards the cross, to hear Jesus at the door more clearly, but, ultimately, he is the only one who can open the door to let Jesus in.

As we attempt to take seriously the other person's problems, blockages and objections, our best course of action is to ask God himself to speak into the situation by asking him to empower us with wisdom to respond to their questions – and better still to reveal himself to them beyond our answers.

GOSPEL PROBLEM QUESTIONS

- If God exists, do you think he is good?
- If I could answer all of your questions about God today, would you want to become a Christian?
- Do you know what Christians believe?
- What do you think happens when we die?
- What do you think is the biggest problem in the world today?

THE GOSPEL POWER QUESTION

'DO YOU BELIEVE IN PRAYER?'

'How did you know that?! How did he know that?!'

The young nightclub promoter was completely bewildered. As he stood talking with me and a couple of my friends on the streets of Magaluf, his confusion wasn't provoked by an overly convoluted explanation of the gospel, but by the fact that I had just spoken very personally into his life with knowledge that I couldn't possibly have had, having only met him five minutes earlier.

While my friends had been chatting with him about the gospel, I had been praying that the Lord might open his heart and lead our conversation. Then, as clear in my mind as recalling a memory from earlier in the day, I became aware that this young guy was having problems with his father.

I gently interrupted my friends who were in full flow with their gospel presentation and said, 'I know this sounds weird, but I think you're having a tough time with your dad right now and God wants you to know that he is your heavenly Father and he loves you and will never abandon you.'

He was stunned.

It turned out that that very morning he had had a huge argument with his dad on the phone and they had said some really hurtful things to each other. The call ended badly and had been playing on his mind all day.

Seeing as he had grown up in the Harry Potter generation, I thought it wise to respond quickly to his confusion before he concluded that I was a wizard and we lost the power of the prophetic moment.

'I don't know anything about you, but God knows everything, and he wanted you to know through me tonight that he loves you. All I did was pray while we were chatting to see if I could speak to you on his behalf tonight. I'll tell you what, why don't we try praying together now and asking God to help in the situation with your dad. If he cares enough to tell you through a stranger that he loves you, I'm sure he can help you with the challenge you're facing with your dad.'

Actually, I was only half joking about him concluding that I was a wizard. Clearly, he wasn't going to think I was an actual wizard, but without clear communication about the source of our power, people can be left with all sorts of confusion and weird ideas about what is really going on. Paul and Barnabas were worshipped as gods by a crowd who witnessed God heal a man through them. Their response was to tear their clothes in lament at this blasphemous misunderstanding and do everything they could to set the people right (Acts 14:8–18). I'm not suggesting you need to start buying your favourite clothes in bulk to allow for dramatic public demonstrations of lament to get your point across, but we definitely need to be just as fervent in pointing people to the true source of our power and hope. Clarity is essential.

Bringing clarity to the other person's confusion is part of the gospel task of bringing peace to chaos. As we offer to pray, we should be clear about who we are praying to and why. We pray to the all-powerful, perfectly good, loving and faithful creator of the universe. We pray to the one true God, who hears our prayers and who is perfectly wise, compassionate and trustworthy to bring the right answer and action in response.

We don't want to give the impression that prayer is some kind of heavenly vending machine from which we can get what we want on demand. Our primary concern in praying with people is that God's glory would be revealed to them so that they might know him, and that the wonder of that most important of all daily prayers could be offered sincerely from their lips for the first time: 'Jesus, please be the Lord of my life today. Forgive me, heavenly Father. Help me, by your Holy Spirit, to live for you and to reveal your glory.'

The club rep agreed to pray and so we prayed together. He said he felt a strange peace that he had never felt before. We shared more of the gospel with him and he decided to take his first steps with Jesus as Lord of his life that very night.

It can be surprising how many people who don't believe in God do believe in prayer in some shape or form, or at the very least are open to the idea of it. But whether or not they say 'yes' to the question, 'Do you believe in prayer?' you can confidently affirm that you do because you believe in the living God who listens to his people. Then, give them examples of how God has worked through prayer in your life. You can ask them if they want to pray right now and what they want to pray about.

If they say 'yes', fantastic – listen to their request and go for it. If they want prayer but are not sure what to pray for, offer some suggestions based on the conversation you've had, or pray for healing if there is an illness. Pray that God would reveal himself in the coming days and weeks to them. Don't promise the kinds of result that cannot be assured (God will do what God will do in his way and in his timing), but don't be afraid to be bold in what you pray for as you leave it in God's hands. Even if we don't see immediate answers to our prayers, we can confidently assert that God is all-powerful (Matthew 19:26), he is perfectly good, loving, kind and trustworthy (Psalm 100:5), he listens to our prayers (1 John 5:14) and he invites us – delights in it, in fact – to turn back to him and pray (2 Chronicles 7:14; Proverbs 15:8).

If they say 'no', then you can ask them if they would mind if you prayed for them in your daily prayers. Explain how you pray each day for various things and that you'd love to add them to that prayer time – after all, what do they have to lose? Make sure you follow through, though – the offer is not a polite gesture but a statement of loving commitment to get God involved in their life through faith-filled prayer!

It's possible some will still say 'no' to this offer, which is fine (and it's possible that they could raise questions about previous unanswered prayer, so perhaps think about how you would respond). You can leave it graciously there in the conversation, but you can still pray for them in your daily prayers and trust the Lord to do with that as he will. My experience has definitely been that, most of the time, people will accept an offer of prayer, and often will be open to be prayed for there and then.

Prayer can really help when it comes to those friends we have known for a long time but with whom we have rarely spoken of Jesus. Starting gospel conversations with these friends can be especially hard. You may feel that suddenly introducing Jesus to an established relationship could come across as something out-of-the-blue or overly 'preachy', and it often feels like there is more at stake in our relationships with our friends than there is in our relationships with a stranger. But offering prayer in response to a situation, challenge or experience a friend shares with you can be a gentle and loving way to bring your faith into your friendship. And through the sincerity of your commitment to prayer, you'll be showing them that far from it being something abnormal or weird, it's one of the most natural aspects of our humanity – spending time in connection with our creator God is quite literally what we were made for!

However it plays out, the gospel power question is an opportunity to talk about and demonstrate the power of God to the other person. And don't miss an opportunity to be the answer to the other person's prayer requests. If they ask for prayer about their loneliness, perhaps you could take the initiative to begin a friendship with them. There are times when God will answer the prayer right in front of you by positioning you to be the answer.

The rest is in his hands, and that – like his power – is the best place for it to be.

GOSPEL POWER QUESTIONS

- Have you ever experienced a miracle?
- Do you believe in the supernatural?
- If God existed, what do you think he would say about you or your life?
- If God could answer one prayer for you today what would it be?
- Have you ever read any of the Bible? If so, what did you think?

THE GOSPEL INVITATION QUESTION

'IS THERE ANYTHING STOPPING YOU FROM PUTTING YOUR TRUST IN JESUS TODAY?'

I once heard the story of a freshly appointed vicar doing the rounds in his new parish, visiting the members of his congregation in their homes. Upon arriving at an elderly couple's house he discovered that, remarkably, they had been attending the church for more than fifty years. As the conversation progressed, he became increasingly aware that they may not actually have been walking in personal faith with Jesus, and so he asked some basic questions to dig a little deeper. Sure enough, it turned out that neither of them had ever committed their life to Christ, even though they had been part of the church community for so many decades.

The young vicar had the joy of leading them through an explanation of the gospel and then asked them if they wanted to put their full trust in Jesus as Lord. The elderly couple were moved to tears by the good news of the gospel and enthusiastically accepted his offer. By the time he left their home, the couple were no longer just churchgoers but adopted and redeemed children of God.

As he said his goodbyes and made his way out, the vicar turned to ask them one last question.

'Can I just ask, why did you wait so long to make this decision?'

The couple looked at each other before the wife responded, plainly: 'Well, no one ever asked us.'

The gospel is an invitation for us to stop running away from God, to repent. As carriers of the gospel, if we miss out this part of the message it's like we are giving someone a parachute and failing to tell them that there's a cord to pull.

Of the many reasons why we can struggle to offer an invitation into relationship with Jesus as part of our personal evangelism, two stand out in particular: squeamishness about repentance and fear of rejection.

Repentance gets a bad rap these days. One too many street preachers have tossed the word around like a conviction sledgehammer, often without offering a helpful explanation of what they really mean. I don't want to be down on street preachers – I know many who I admire greatly for their boldness and compassion – but sometimes we need to take a step back and see that some of our methods may have been lacking and should be rethought a little here and there, especially where the method obscures our message.

No matter the connotations we might carry for the word, 'repentance' simply means 'turn around, you're going the wrong way.'

The good news of what Jesus has done for the world is that, despite our rebellion which leads to death today and forever, we can turn back to God and know his life today and forever. Our sin is our rejection of God – the author of life, goodness and love. The call of Jesus in his preaching was to turn back to God; the action of Jesus on the cross was the way by which all could do so. He took the punishment for our sin upon himself, and made it possible for us to be washed clean from the chaos and catastrophe of our rebellion (Mark 1:15; Romans 6:23; Romans 10:9; 1 Peter 2:24–25).

Too many have caricatured the message of repentance as a 'turn or burn' ultimatum, and because of the stark nature of such a proclamation it has fallen out of fashion to bring it up at all. We want others to know about how much Jesus loves them, but would rather skirt around that awkward stuff about sin and repentance. Surely we can be the ones to let them know about God's love, and then God could tell them about the tricky sin stuff in a dream or something, when we're long gone?

No deal.

We don't have to bulldoze our way into conversations by screaming 'turn or burn' at people, but we do need to make it clear that God is looking for a response to his love and his holiness. The only appropriate response is to repent. It's not just about being saved from hell – permanent separation from God – but turning around from walking in death and stepping into true, Jesus-centred life today.

The other reason we shy away from inviting people into a relationship with Jesus is the possibility of rejection. None of us enjoy being rejected. It's nearly always an unpleasant experience. The problem with asking someone a direct question like, 'Do you want to become a Christian?' is that it opens us up to rejection. But there's no getting away from it – invitation is a core element of evangelism. We must invite people into relationship with Jesus, and inevitably that will mean we face some rejection along the way.

When Samuel had his ego wounded by the Israelites' desire to have an earthly king lead them, God gently reminded him that their rejection was not of Samuel's leadership but of God's own leadership as the King of kings (1 Samuel 8:7). Don't take rejection of the gospel personally. Rejection of the gospel is a rejection of God before it is a rejection of you, and he is not dismayed. He continues to lovingly extend his grace to all who would have ears to hear and eyes to see his truth. He does not grow weary. And, in his strength, we too can endure rejections for the hope of the world and for his glory.

The 'how' and 'when' of arriving at the moment of invitation will vary from opportunity to opportunity. I've found that the easiest way by far is to simply ask a question like: 'Is there anything stopping you from putting your trust in Jesus today?' This 'pre-invitation' question is a little check to see if the road is clear for a more direct invitation to place their trust in Jesus, to see whether the other person is ready to take the next step. And before you can ask this question, you will need to ensure you have explained enough of the gospel for it to mean something.

If their answer is 'Yes, there is something,' then see if you can work through the issue conversationally, prayerfully, graciously and gently. Don't try to quickly resolve the issue so you can get the deal done! Some things will take time, which is another reminder of why ongoing relationship is so important to personal evangelism.

If the answer is 'No', then you can joyfully lead them through taking the next step of making Jesus Lord of their life there and then, and point them towards the next steps.

When I talk to people about Jesus, I expect a response for two reasons. Firstly, I believe that God is powerful enough to work a miracle of restoration and redemption in any person's life – even through me with all my rough edges and weakness. Secondly, because I always ask for some kind of response! I always offer some kind of invitation. Can I pray for you? Can we meet up again? Will you go to this discipleship course? Will you take this Bible away and read that section? These are all good invitations. I don't want to be pushy – and feedback from various polls suggests that many people appreciate faith conversations without an overly confrontational moment of decision – but I do want to offer some kind of next step, even if it's as simple as a friendly invitation for the person to keep thinking about the things we've discussed.

But then there are the times when it all comes together by God's grace and the best of all invitations can be made, the invitation that I always long to extend above all others:

Is there anything stopping you from putting your trust in Jesus today?

No?

Well then, would you like to accept Jesus as Lord of your life?

God invites you to partner with him today to invite those who don't yet know him into the relationship they were created for, that they may know life today and that he may be eternally glorified.

It's time for us to joyfully take up the invitation of our God to go. Let's humbly and boldly ask the world some life-bringing questions.

GOSPEL INVITATION QUESTIONS

- Would you be interested in meeting up again?
- Would you be interested in going to church?
- Do you have a Bible? Would you like one? Would you be interested in reading together?
- Is there anything I can do to help you take the step of faith to follow Jesus?
- Do you want to accept Jesus as Lord of your life?

A FINAL NOTE ABOUT GOOD CONVERSATION

I hope the suggested questions and ideas from this little book are helpful to you as you head into the world and engage in conversations with those around you. But before you go, it's worth mentioning a few final pointers to help keep your conversations healthy and holy.

First of all, make sure you don't interrogate your conversation partner. It's all too easy to turn what starts out as a friendly chat into a re-enactment of the Spanish inquisition. In my experience people don't enjoy being interrogated! The questions in this book are designed to get a conversation going, or keep one flowing in an engaging, relational and Jesus-centred way, not to expose people to an off-putting and rigorous existential examination. We needn't force them onto the back foot through well-intentioned but misguidedly zealous evangelistic duty. With that in mind…

Keep the conversation open. Don't try to force the conversation down roads it doesn't want to travel. Be careful not to ask overly personal and intrusive questions with people you've only just met. Even something as simple as, 'What do you do for a living?' can be perceived as intrusive (and reductive). Keep it simple and general to begin with and see where it goes. If the other person doesn't seem comfortable or open to the questions you ask or ideas you raise, feel free to talk about other things. Not every moment of every conversation needs to be a strategic conversational chess move towards kingdom revelation! Sometimes talking about the weather (I'm British so all of my conversations start this way), a sports result from the previous night, or a non-intrusive enquiry ('I see you're reading *XYZ*, is it good?'; 'Oh I love those shoes, where could I get some like that?') are all perfectly natural conversational starters. They're all topics that serve no purpose beyond developing affinity (shout out to my cute dog Toshi and my tattoos for being regular conversation sparks for other people towards me), but can provide a great opportunity for a deeper topic. You don't need to attempt to save the world in a single conversation. Just chat, be open to gospel opportunity as it arises and intentional about it when it does. Speaking of intentionality...

Delight in hospitality. Go out of your way to be generously hospitable. Invite people to your home, for food at a restaurant, to hang out in a coffee shop. Don't just invite them to church, invite them to spend time with you in your life, take care of their need via a good meal, bless them with personal fellowship. Hospitality was central to Jesus' ministry and it should be central to the life of the church today. Our goal is not to lure someone onto our turf so that we can soften them up for a gospel-slap-in-the-face moment, but to simply love people with our time, with food, with a listening ear and with good company. From this generosity and love, opportunity to speak of Jesus will naturally flow, and will increase over time wherever authentic and lasting relationship develops.

And as it does, make sure you know your own story. Be ready to share how God has been at work in your life – not just in the moment you first decided to follow Jesus, but this month, this week, today. We should always be aware not to make ourselves the centre of the conversation (listening well is still an absolute priority), and careful not to over-relate our own experiences to theirs, but there will be times when it is good and right (a holy moment of opportunity) to give witness to God's work in your life, relying on his Spirit to empower your witness as you share (Acts 1:8).

Sometimes it can be helpful to explicitly ask permission to share your faith with the person you're speaking with. You might say something like, 'It's so interesting to hear about your experiences, thank you for sharing with me. Would you mind if I shared about how my relationship with God has helped me through similar challenges?' This can help to avoid putting people on the back foot when Jesus makes a sudden appearance in the conversation. Mostly, though, this is another way to show considerate care to the other person. In my experience people say 'yes' more often than not, and usually with a softer heart to receive the truth you share.

It's okay to disagree in a conversation. Disagreement doesn't need to result in animosity. We can avoid overreacting to counter positions, even where they threaten to offend. Ask God to help you be measured, kind and clear in response. It's not about winning arguments, but people. It's hard for someone to be impacted by the peace of Jesus when they're busy pulling out the shrapnel of the disagreement grenade we used to make our point with a bigger bang than theirs. Time brings perspective, so when you hit an impasse, create space by moving to another topic, or another conversation another day, so you can both consider the disagreement without the pressure of having to come up with an immediate response. Refresh your emotional state, and then talk again.

Finally, let us remember that Jesus' commissioning words remind us that not only do we step into these conversations by his exclusive and total authority, but also in his powerful and transforming presence (Matthew 28:18–20). We are to be a transformed and empowered people carrying the transformational and empowering message of Jesus into the world, with one ultimate question in mind:

Do you know him?

EVANGELISM RESOURCES

BOOKS ABOUT THE GOSPEL

Recovering The Real Lost Gospel, Darryl Bock (B&H Academic, 2010)

What Is The Gospel, Greg Gilbert (Crossway, 2010)

The Simple Gospel, Ben Jack (The Message Trust, 2018)

The King Jesus Gospel, Scot McKnight (Zondervan, 2016 revised ed.)

Simply Good News, Tom Wright (SPCK, 2015)

METHODS OF EXPLAINING THE GOSPEL

Who Am I? (advancegroups.org)

Jesus At The Door (jesusatthedoor.com)

The Three Circles (various YouTube examples)

The 4 Points (The4Points.com)

Two Ways To Live (twowaystolive.com)

3, 2, 1: The Story of God, The World and You (three-two-one.org)

Wordless Book (letthelittlechildrencome.com)

OTHER PRACTICAL BOOKS ABOUT EVANGELISM

Conversational Evangelism, Norman and David Geisler (Harvest House, 2009)

Big Yes, Little Yes, Healthy Maybe, Mark Greenwood (Verite CM, 2019)

Here I Am: Joining God's Adventurous Call To Love The World, Andy Hawthorne (David C. Cook, 2019)

Story Bearer, Phil Knox (IVP, 2020)

The Introverted Evangelist, Reuben Morley (Verite CM, 2020)

Questioning Evangelism, Randy Newman (Kregel Publications, 2018)

Evangelism, J. Mack Stiles (Crossway, 2014)

Honest Evangelism, Rico Tice (The Good Book Company, 2015)

CONVERSING WITH OTHER FAITHS

Engaging With... A series of short books from the Good Book Company about engaging with other faiths.

ONLINE & COURSE RESOURCES

Advance Groups (advancegroups.org)

The Bible Project (bibleproject.com)

The Alpha Course (alpha.org)

Christianity Explored (christianityexplored.org)

The Bible Course (biblesociety.org.uk)

Talking Jesus (talkingjesus.org)

ABOUT THE AUTHOR

Ben Jack is the global head of Advance, based at The Message Trust (message.org.uk) in Manchester, England. Ben travels the world to preach the gospel and encourage and equip others to do likewise. He is the author of *My Lord and My God*, *The Simple Gospel* and *The Advance Group Mentoring Guide*, and has been known to produce music and tour as DJ Galactus Jack. Ben and his wife Naomi live in Manchester with their pug Toshi.

THE GOSPEL. THERE IS NO PLAN B.

The gospel is good news to be proclaimed and has lost none of its power to save. Through small group mentoring, Advance equips, encourages and empowers the church in evangelism while also stirring and developing evangelistic gifting in those called as evangelists.

Advance grew out of a commitment by British and American evangelists Andy Hawthorne (The Message Trust) and Andrew Palau (Luis Palau Association) to gather up to twelve younger preaching evangelists in small group community to intentionally develop and sharpen them. Since its inception in 2015, Advance has grown from the first group in Manchester, UK, to a global movement of hundreds of groups meeting regularly around the world who are committed to fanning into flame the gift of God in their lives that the world may know him.

FIVE PRINCIPLES OF THE MOVEMENT

- ⏱ Regular meeting
- ✂ Sharpening
- 🔊 Accountability
- 💬 Communication
- ✳ Multiplication

Advance exists to increase and equip the number of Christians who will unashamedly put the lamp of the gospel on a stand around the globe, be it from a platform or through daily encounters with family, friends or even strangers.

Discover more and sign up to start a group:

ADVANCEGROUPS.ORG

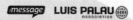

GLOBAL NETWORK
OF ≡VANGELISTS

SO THAT ALL MAY HEAR //

One evangelist can reach only so far. One organization can do only so much. By working together, we multiply our efforts for the expansion of the Gospel. This is the vision of our Global Network of Evangelists.

Dedicating the next decade to accelerate evangelism worldwide, the Palau Association is working to build networks of evangelists in 150 countries. These networks are being developed through strong, trusted relationships with evangelists and Christian organizations around the globe, with a vision to connect and encourage evangelists as never before to win more people to Christ.

This Global Network of Evangelists is using all available means to annually reach millions with the good news of Jesus Christ. What God is doing through this outstanding network of evangelists is truly astounding.

LUIS PALAU

Through mentoring and equipping, collaborative outreach events, and training and conferences, members are provided with the help they need to impact their world for Christ. Our plan is to extend this offering to thousands more evangelists from around the world, forming the first-ever global network, spread across 150+ countries.

evangelist.global

DISCOVER THE ADVANCE
PROCLAIMERS SERIES

Equipping the Church

Equipping the Church exists to do just that, equip the church for all areas of ministry.

If you are an evangelist, you, and anyone else in your church with any area of responsibility and leadership, can become an Equip member and receive the following long term benefits:

- 20% off orders in-store and online.*
- Special offers at event bookstores
- Regular e-newsletters about new church resources
- Seasonal brochures highlighting key books and resources

*some exclusions apply, such as packs that are already discounted and some sale items

This scheme is designed to help you access the best resources to equip you and your church for ministry and evangelism.

Please go to **www.equippingthechurch.com/equip** to sign up now!

"SO THAT THE SERVANT OF GOD MAY BE THOROUGHLY EQUIPPED FOR EVERY GOOD WORK."
2 TIMOTHY 3:17